Serendipitous Me

Nilanjana Sengupta

BookLeaf Publishing

India | USA | UK

Made with ❤ on the BookLeaf Publishing Platform
www.bookleafpub.in
www.bookleafpub.com

Dedication

For all those who believe in Life to be an Experiential
Journey &
seek validation nowhere else but within....

Preface

This Book was a Serendipity
It is an anthology of poems that reflect myriad emotions
These poems were written in different points in time
Hope the reader resonates at some level with my words

Acknowledgements

I am filled with a deep sense of gratitude towards the Universe for being an enabler for me to experience life with all its Highs & Lows and for making my journey so far both Eventful & Meaningful

Thank You to all those people who have been a meaningful part of this Journey called LIFE...

1. Known meets the Unknown

Woke up to the call of the sea
Splashing water making sound
Reminding of the treasures unfound
The treasures nicely wrapped and kept safe
Only those who live true to their spirit
Can reach that place
Priceless it is yet it never comes free
The free spirited knows the art to discover and unravel it
for the world to experience it and see
When I look beyond
I can see no boundary
For nothing can be bound
Only the one who wants to live it fully
Will be able to find the unfound
The journey is endless
The destination unknown
I set myself free again
For it is a journey to know the unknown.....

2. Rain of Reason

In the midst of the humdrum..I forgot who I was..
I looked inwards..and went for a pause..
The inner crevices were screeching aloud..
The light of reasoning was lost in the cloud..
I looked once more and tried again
To see if I could set the clouds aside
And bring some rain..
It is the rain that makes you dance
The rain that brings back hope
The rain that cleanses the dirt
That clouds thy mind and soul
It is the rain that brings back reason
And makes you sing in glee
As you inner fears and doubts vanish into thee
When at last I could set the clouds aside
And bring some rain of reason
My life changed along
Like the change of a season
At last It rained and it rained to set me free
The rain of reason could again let me be...

3. The Star

Dreaming to
Shine like a star
Standing afar
Frightened to reveal
Who it is
For the world
Might rip it apart
Crestfallen heart
Trying to find a start
Undying are the nerves
Pushing inch by inch
Even with the broken wings
Lunging out breath
Taking another step
With a hope to meet thee
Where everything will be true
And the spirit will be free
Where colors will be real
And faces won't fake smiles
Where truth will reign supreme

And the efforts will bear fruits with sheen
Where hands will be there to help
At a call cry or yelp
Far fetched it may all seem
But there is no censor to one's dream
Daring are those who dream to live the good
And time shall also favour those
Who dared to stand tall & withstood

4. Lost

Silence penetrating the walls
And when that happens
Time would unfailingly stall
Hollow passages without the sound
Of anyone passing by
Only the beating of the heart you can clearly hear if you
try
People known and related are many
But in times like these
You seldom remember any
Your own company engulfing you
Not in warmth but in solitude
A frozen mind
Faltering steps
Struggling to establish identity
To match with the world
Approved steps
Blurred vision
Thoughtless mind
In times like these

You are just a body
Who lost its soul in time...

5. Christmas Gift

On the eve of Christmas
As I sit by the Christmas tree
Thinking about life
And all that I got from it for free
Reminiscing my childhood that held promises galore
With the adulthood at its peak
The wonderland is left ashore
Many years swept by
The longing did not die
To meet the one who would be by my
side when I say my last goodbye
Some people say I am a buffoon
For I did not realise soon
That life is everything but a fairytale
Where everyone is striving to have their sail
Through the storms that may rock you
but will not shatter
Saving what's best for you for the latter

Latter it is that I am waiting for
The only Christmas Gift that I wish for
To find what is mine before it is time
To say my Final Goodbye !!!

6. My Sunflower

Shining bright in the morning light
Every morning I yearn for its sight
Test of time alone withstood
Not once did it ask for help
Even when it could
I wish I were there by its side
Holding its hand tight
Through all its fight
I wish I could have shared its pain
When it stood out alone in the rain
I wish I could have tended to its wounds
So that they would have healed soon
I lament at my fate for I couldn't be there
When it needed me the most
It was all alone in despair
Now that I have found it in my garden again
I would forever be by its side
Not let it out of my sight
For I cannot lose my Sunflower Again.

7. Finding Me

Been some time
that My words would rhyme
Lost in time
Did it lose its shine
Or is it the memory doing its part
What Matters it keeps
What doesn't it throws apart
Or is it life changing its hues
What mattered before is old
May be it is the time to look for something new
Something that would lend shape to the wandering
thoughts
& revive the lost spirit from its distraught
Sometimes numbness feels like being dead
Fearful of none
Treading that step without the dread
The dread of losing it all & then finding
The real me
For is this life not a chase or a maze
To find ,which seldom one can

In spite of the never ending spree

8. Heaven's Gate

Mind clouded by the material clout
Failing to hear the wails the cries
& the incessant shout
The shout of the soul that is pained & hurt
A struggle to live through all the dirt
Purgatory is it ?? this life???
Whose onus is it to set it all right
Or is it an illusion to scrape through it all
foreseeable it is the Inevitable fall
Loss or Gain would not be any
Reality is an escape not for a few but many
Chosen are the ones who
Live by faith
More in self to reach that state
Where it would all make sense
Whether early or late
Before they reach the heaven's gate

9. Know Thyself

Genuine at heart
Open in views
Frank with words
Understood by few
Often mistaken
Taken for granted
Hesitant to face the world
Feeling unwanted
Neither a big house
Nor a big car
The things that fancy the world
Did not gladden the heart
Caring words
Genuine concern
An acknowledgment of self
Was needed to reaffirm
Search continued
Disappointments were many
Till a voice within spoke..
"Look for acknowledgment within

Look for care within
Show yourself the concern that you look for outside..
And only then will you be able to give all that back to
the world where you came from
And in return receive all that you had always longed for
in a magnitude beyond measure.."

10. An Unsolved Mystery

An unsolved mystery
Written in history
Knocking the doors of the mind
Where darkness unfathomable one could find
Charting the narrow alleys in search of light
That would put an end to that plight
Tireless striving with a hope
That there still lies a scope
To heal the wounds & rise again
For No effort ever goes in vain
Winning and losing are all in the mind
Meaningful they live whose hearts are kind
For Life is lived in deeds and not in years
And the ones who live it for real earn the cheers

11. If only

Broken & Beaten
But wasn't out
No one was there to help
none heard thy shout
A cry for help was it or no
It certainly wasn't a regular show
Nerves were wrecked
Pain was none
Numbed core
Knew no one
Braved the darkness
Light was unseen
Outward though it looked pristine
Years went by toughening the core
Wounds weren't fresh
But they felt sore
Beaten & broken
But wasn't out
If only
Someone had heard thy shout...

12. A place you can call your own

Idea of life as we live it strikes no different to people &
they all believe it to be true
Stereotype is the good nemesis, anything otherwise is
disapproved
Trials are none, just the hapless heart
Longing to put it all to an end
Regrets and sorrows the heart holds none
Rhyming it all too sounds like a pun
Living the life on the edge without a fence
Worrying that this too might be an offence
to those who live by the written rules
And those who don't being mocked as fools
With no hopes to live in a world that
Doesn't see the outliers as one of their own
A flickering candle of hope is
somewhere still alight
Putting up its solo fight not against the world but its
own
Trying hard to make a place that can be called its own

13. You meet you

The hustle of the daily routine
Takes you further away from you
With an outward facade to look pristine
Makes you forget the real you
The race you lose yourself to
Takes you nowhere worthwhile
The prime time of life is swished away
Erasing the memory of being infantile
Real happiness is not in ranks titles or fame
The efforts relentless would all be in vain
Halt pause reflect for a moment
To understand the real you
For even for a moment if you meet yourself
Your purpose in life will be met
In not people places power but within you...

14. Soulmate

Your soul to mine
Running amok in history
Telling a story in time
Heart skipping its beat
Walking alone in that empty street
Questions many
Answers few
Courage lost somewhere
To know the truth
Time it took to unburden the past
And a new day awaited at last
To give a chance to the lost hope
Seizing the moment to make a scope
To relive the dreams lost in time
And to learn again to make the words rhyme...

15. Forever by your side

When the world looks gloomy
And the heart skips its beat
When the way seems lost
And the floor is off your feet
When tiresome it gets
And the vision seems blurred
When everything seems unreal
And your heart is hurt
Turn inwards
And go for a pause
Quieten your mind
And look for the cause
If you look with intent
Your answer will be there
You would hear the voice telling you
"You are not alone
I am there
I am in you and
With you
You are tired I know

as you have been searching for me long
Don't worry it's all worth
Now that you know I was there with you all along
When nothing seems to work
And the days are not bright
Look inside with hope
You will never lose my sight
I am the love I am the peace
I am the friend that never leaves
I shall Forever be by your side
If you set aside your doubts
And look for me inside"

16. Self-Love

Beaten but not broken
Time tested seasons were many
Standing alone and withstanding it all
Shed not one tear but many
The spirit put up its fight
with all the darkness
Looming by the sight
Fought the self-doubts
That held thou back from the
Awaited flight
When at last the shackles were broken
& thou soared high in the sky
With the new found love for self
Gleefully flew higher & higher in the sky

17. One Day

Yearning for the day
When love will win over hate
When we will lift each other up
Instead of making fun of someone's helpless state
When happiness will be in sharing and caring
When success of the other will feel like one's own
When shedding all inhibitions to express one's true
feelings
We will set out to fly on our own
When judgments will be for justice
And not to put each other down
When peace will reign supreme in lives of all
It will then be that time
When victor will be the Good
& Admitting its defeat Evil would fall!!!!

18. Broken

beaten roads
broken heart
worn out soles
gone miles afar
Questions were many
answers were few
like the rarest season
Of the morning dew
Little did i know
That it would pain so much
If I knew
I would have never let it out of my clutch

19. Gift of Time

Rising from the ashes
Burnt to grey
Looking for another chance
with a will to stay
Stumbled many times
The wounds bled too
Yet the journey continued sans pause
As there was a lot to do
Can't tell the month year or the day
A lot of Time had passed
Yet none of that would make it sway
Knowing a long portion of the journey had long passed
Though many a milestones were strewn ahead
The soul moved undeterred
No matter how hard it was
It seemed worth all the pain
For in life it knew well
That there lay
no gain without the pain
No efforts made would ever go in vain

It's one life & you have to find the treasure
Which was securely placed in that lane
The journey would end one day to the lane where the
treasure laid
The pain would by then have lessened
And the memories would even fade
What would remain would be the spirit of content
That it was a life well lived
With nothing to regret for or repent
Not many get the chance
To find that hidden treasure
But the ones who do
Are privileged to experience this pleasure
So why not we try to
Live our best life in this one lifetime
& May be we could be the chosen one
To experience the real gift of time....

20. Attraction

An element of intrigue
The mystical charm
Conquered thy soul
And left thou unarmed
The timelessness of space
The sudden pause
Little did thou realise
The whirlwind's cause

21. I am Human

I am not mad
I am human
I make mistakes
I am human
I get angry
I am human
I am tender
I am human
I feel pain
I am human
I get lost
I am human
I am not always right
I am human
I annoy you
I am human
I hurt you
I am human
I get hurt
I am human

It is the inconsistency of my being that makes me more
human than i can be
So human I am;
Human I will be
Rules do not define me
I make my rules
My karma is my doing
The good in me will bring me more good
And the part that isn't will leave me
With an experience richer
Than any other!

www.ingramcontent.com/pod-product-compliance
Lightning Source LLC
LaVergne TN
LVHW010952200726
843509LV00013B/2388